*The*

# STORY

*of*

## Christmas

THE
PASSION
TRANSLATION

**BroadStreet**

Scripture text translated from the original Hebrew, Greek, and
Aramaic texts by Dr. Brian Simmons.

See www.thepassiontranslation.com for all books available.

Published by BroadStreet Publishing Group, LLC
Racine, Wisconsin, USA
www.broadstreetpublishing.com

Cover design by Chris Garborg at www.garborgdesign.com
Interior by Katherine Lloyd at www.theDESKonline.com

Printed in the United States of America

15  16  17  18  19  20    10  9  8  7  6  5  4  3  2  1

# Contents

# Introduction

*E*very good story offers a great promise. The story of Christmas is no different. It speaks into the hopelessness and restlessness of our day by revealing a God who has been on mission to save us.

From the beginning of our human story, God promised a Rescuer who would come to fix our brokenness. When he made good on that promise, he did so in an unexpected way: by sending his Son, the Anointed One! He is the Savior who lives in us, the King who will return for us.

You are invited to experience this story, and unwrap the promises it offers you and your world.

*The*
# STORY
*of*
## Christmas

For many, Christmas is so hopeful because life can be so hopeless. It wasn't supposed to be like this, though. In the beginning God made everything very good. Then our ancestors ruined it all. Yet God didn't given up on us! From the very beginning he's been on mission to rescue us. God promised a Child-King who would establish his kingdom realm, bring light to the darkness, establish justice on earth, and suffer to heal us all. Thankfully God made good on his promise!

## *A Child Is Promised*
GENESIS 3:14–15

The Lord God said to the serpent ... "I will cause a dire hostility to exist between you and the woman, and between your children and her children. And he will render a crushing blow to your head even though you will strike her children's heel."

## *King of the World*
PSALM 96

Go ahead—sing your new song to the Lord!
Let everyone in every language
   sing him a new song.
Don't stop! Keep on singing!
Make his name famous!
Tell everyone every day how wonderful he is!
Give them the good news of our great Savior.
Take the message of his glory and miracles
   to every nation.
Tell them about all the amazing things
   he has done.
For the Lord's greatness is beyond description
and he deserves all the praise
   that comes to him.
He is our King-God and it's right to be
   in holy awe of him.
Other gods are absolutely worthless.

For the Lord God is Creator God
  who spread the splendor of the skies!
Breathtaking brilliance and awe-inspiring majesty
radiate from his shining presence.
His stunning beauty overwhelms all who come
  before him!
Surrender to the Lord Yahweh all you nations
  and peoples.
Surrender to him all your pride and strength.
Confess that Jehovah alone deserves all the
  glory and honor!
Bring an offering and come celebrate
  in his courts.
Come worship the Lord God wearing
  the splendor of holiness.
Let everyone wait in wonder as they tremble
  in awe before him.
Tell the nations plainly that Yahweh
  rules over all!
He is doing a great job, and nothing will
  disrupt him,
for he treats everyone fair and square.
Let the skies sing for joy!
Let the earth join in the chorus.
Let oceans thunder and fields echo this
  ecstatic praise
until every swaying tree of every forest joins in,

lifting up their songs of joyous praise to him!
For here he comes, the Lord God,
and he's ready to judge the world.
He will do what's right and can be trusted to
   always do what's fair!

### Messiah, King, and Priest
PSALM 110:1–4

Jehovah-God said to my Lord, the Messiah:
"Sit with me as Enthroned Ruler
while I subdue your every enemy.
They will bow low before you
as I make them a footstool for your feet!"
Messiah, I know God himself will establish
   your kingdom
as you reign in Zion-glory.
For he says to you: "Rule in the midst of your
   enemies!"
Your people will be your love offerings
like living sacrifices spilled out before you!
In the day of your mighty power
   you will be exalted,
and in the brightness of your holy ones
you will shine as an army arising
from the dawning rays of a new day,
anointed with the dew of your youth!
Jehovah-God has taken a solemn oath

and will never back away from it, saying:
"You are a priest for eternity, my King of
     righteousness!"

### A Virgin Will Conceive
ISAIAH 7:10–14

The Lord spoke through Isaiah again and said to
King Ahaz: "Go ahead—ask for a sign from the Lord
your God! Make your request beyond the realm of
possibility! Ask for something miraculous!"

But Ahaz replied, "I don't want to ask or to chal-
lenge the Lord to a test."

So Isaiah said to him, "Listen, O house of David:
Is it not enough that you try my patience? Must you
also try the patience of my God? Therefore, the
Sovereign Lord himself will choose the sign he gives
you—a virgin will carry a child and will give birth to
a son! And you will name him, God-With-Us!"

### The Darkness Turns to Light
ISAIAH 9:2–7

I will dispel all gloom for those who are fearful of
judgment! Although the Lord once greatly humbled the region of Zebulon and Naphtali, he will
one day bestow upon them great honor—from the
Mediterranean eastward to the other side of the
Jordan, and throughout the Galilee of the Gentiles.

For the people who walked in darkness will see

a radiant light shining upon them—illuminating even the darkest places. They once lived in the shadows of death, but now a brilliant light is shining on them.

Lord you have given them overflowing joy and made them happy! They are ecstatic over what you have done, rejoicing as those who bring in a great harvest and like those who divide up the plunder they have captured.

For God will break the chains that bind his people and lifted off the bar across their shoulders and the rod the oppressor used on them. You have shattered all their bondage, just like you did when Midian's armies were defeated!

Every boot of troops on the march, every uniform caked in blood is destined to be burned as fuel for the fire.

A child has been born for us! A son has been given to us! The responsibility of total dominion rests on his shoulders. And he will be known as: The Wonderful One! The Marvelous Counselor! The Mighty God! The Father of Eternity! And The Prince of Peace!

His kingdom authority will be great and he will bring immeasurable prosperity! He will rule on David's throne and establish David's kingdom from this time forward and for evermore. He will continue to strengthen it by promoting righteousness and justice! The Lord's great passion for his people will insure that it is finished.

### The Branch from Jesse
ISAIAH 11:1-5

A branch will spring forth from Jesse's cut off stump and a shoot will sprout from his roots. The Spirit of Yahweh will be placed upon him—the Spirit of Skillful Wisdom and the Spirit of Profound Understanding, the Spirit of Wise Counsel and the Spirit of Mighty Power, the Spirit of Revelation and the Spirit of the Fear of the Lord. And he will take all his delight in living in the fear of the Lord. He will not judge merely by how things appear or make his decisions on the basis of hearsay. He will uphold justice for the poor and defend the lowly of the earth. His words will be like a scepter that strikes the earth and with his breath he will slay the wicked. Justice will be his waistband and faithfulness his belt.

### The Promise-Keeping Lord
ISAIAH 30:18

The Lord is still waiting for you to come home to him so he can show you his amazing love. And like he promised, he will conquer you to bless you. For the Lord is always faithful to his promises. Those who entwine their hearts with him, waiting for him to help them will be overwhelmed with bliss!

### The Servant of the Lord

ISAIAH 42:1-7

See, this is my servant whom I strengthen and take hold of. He is my chosen one, for in him I find all my delight. I have placed my Spirit on him; he will decree justice to spring up for the nations. He will be gentle and will not be found yelling at others in public. He would never crush a broken heart, or extinguish a flickering flame, but he will faithfully make just decrees. His inner being will never be broken, nor his light grow dim before he establishes justice on the earth. And even the distant lands beyond the seas will hunger for his instruction.

### The Suffering Servant

ISAIAH 52:13-53:12

Look! My servant will prosper and succeed! He will be highly honored, raised up high, and greatly exalted! Just as many were appalled at the sight of him, for he was disfigured and marred, and no longer looked like a man, so now he will astonish and sprinkle many peoples. Kings will be shocked and speechless before him. For what was never told them they now see, and things unheard of now fill their thoughts.

Who could have ever believed what we just heard? And to whom has Yahweh's mighty power been revealed?

He sprouted up like a tender sapling before the Lord, rooted in parched soil. He possessed no distinguishing beauty or outward majesty to catch our attention—nothing special in his appearance to make us follow after him.

He was despised and rejected by others; a man who experienced sorrows and was no stranger to suffering. We turned our faces away from him in disgust and considered him not worthy of respect.

Yet he was the one who carried our diseases and endured the torment of our sufferings. We viewed him as one who was being punished for something he had done, struck down by God and brought low.

But it was because of our rebellious deeds that he was pierced and because of our sins that he was crushed. He endured the punishment that made us well and his bruises have brought us healing.

Like wandering sheep we have all gone astray. Each of us have left God's paths and chosen our own. And the Lord has laid the guilt of all our sins upon him.

He was treated harshly, still he humbly submitted; refusing to defend himself. He was led like a lamb to be slaughtered. Like a silent sheep before his shearers, he didn't even open his mouth.

It was after an unjust trial that he was led away and no one seemed to care. He was cut down in the prime of life; because of the rebellion of his own people he was struck down.

They were going to bury him with criminals, but instead, he ended up in a rich man's tomb because he had done no violence, nor spoken falsely.

Yet it was the will of God to crush him with pain. But once restitution was made, he will be restored to favor and gaze upon his many offspring, prolonging his days. And the Lord's perfect plan will be fully accomplished through him.

After his painful life he will see light and be satisfied. By knowing him, my servant will pronounce over many: "Innocent," for he carried away their sins.

So I will assign him a portion among a great and powerful multitude and with mighty ones he will divide the spoils of victory—all because he poured out his life-blood to death. He was counted as just one of the rebels, yet he carried sin's burden for many and interceded on behalf of the rebels.

### *The Righteous Branch*
JEREMIAH 23:5–6

Listen! I, the Lord, promise you that a time is coming when I will raise up a righteous Branch who will sprout from David's lineage. And he will rule as King, and his reign will prosper with wisdom and understanding. He will succeed in bringing justice and righteousness to all. Under his rule Judah and Israel will be kept safe and secure. And he will be known by this name: The LORD, Our Righteousness!

### *The Coming of Zion's King*
ZECHARIAH 9:9–10

Daughter of Zion, let your joy be great! Daughter of Jerusalem, shout your praises! For here comes your King! Look! He is fully qualified to save you and bring you victory! Yet he comes to you humbly, riding on the back of a donkey—sitting on a young donkey, a young foal of a female donkey...Then he will proclaim peace to the nations and his dominion will be from sea to sea—from the Great River to the ends of the earth!

### *Angelic Prophecy of Jesus' Birth*
LUKE 1:26–38

During the sixth month of Elizabeth's pregnancy, the angel Gabriel was sent from God's presence to an unmarried girl named Miriam, living in Nazareth, a village in Galilee. She was engaged to a man named Joseph, a true descendant of King David. Gabriel appeared to her and said, "Grace to you, young woman, for the Lord is with you and so you are anointed with great favor."

Miriam was shocked over the words of the angel and bewildered over what this may mean for her. But the angel reassured her, saying, "Do not yield to your fear, Miriam, for the Lord has found delight in you and has chosen to surprise you with a wonderful gift. You will become pregnant with a baby boy, and you are to name him Jesus. He will be supreme and will be known as the Son of the Highest. And the Lord God will enthrone him as King on his ancestor David's throne. He will reign as King of Israel forever, and his reign will have no limit."

Miriam said, "But how could this happen? I am still a virgin!"

Gabriel answered, "The Spirit of Holiness will fall upon you and the almighty God will spread his shadow of power over you in a cloud of glory! This is why the child born to you will be holy, and he will be called the Son of God. What's more, your aged aunt, Elizabeth, has also became pregnant with a son. The 'barren one' is now in her sixth month.

Not one promise from God is empty of power, for with God there is no such thing as impossibility!"

Then Miriam responded, saying, "This is amazing! I will be a mother for the Lord! As his servant, I accept whatever he has for me. May everything you have told me come to pass." And the angel left her.

### Elizabeth's Prophecy to Miriam
LUKE 1:39–56

Afterward, Miriam arose and hurried off to the hill country of Judea, to the village where Zechariah and Elizabeth lived. Arriving at their home, Miriam entered the house and greeted Elizabeth. At the moment she heard Miriam's voice, the baby within Elizabeth's womb jumped and kicked. And suddenly, Elizabeth was filled to overflowing with the Holy Spirit! With a loud voice she *prophesied with power*:

Miriam! You are a woman given
    the highest favor
and privilege above all others.
For your child is destined to bring God
    great delight.
How did I deserve such a remarkable honor
to have the mother of my Lord come and visit me?

The moment you came in the door and
  greeted me,
my baby danced inside me with ecstatic joy!
Great favor is upon you, for you have believed
every word spoken to you from the Lord.

## Miriam's Prophetic Song

And Miriam sang this song:

My soul is ecstatic, overflowing with praises
  to God!
My spirit bursts with joy over my life-giving God!
For he set his tender gaze upon me,
  his lowly servant girl.
And from here on, everyone will know
that I have been favored and blessed.
The Mighty One has worked a mighty
  miracle for me;
holy is his name!
Mercy kisses all his godly lovers,
from one generation to the next.
Mighty power flows from him
to scatter all those who walk in pride.
Powerful princes he tears from their thrones
and he lifts up the lowly *to take their place*.
Those who hunger for him will always be filled,
but the smug and self-satisfied he will send
  away empty.

Because he can never forget to show mercy,
he has helped his chosen servant, Israel,
keeping his promises to Abraham
and to his descendants forever.

Before going home, Miriam stayed with Elizabeth for about three months.

# The
# STORY
## of
# Christmas

For generations the people of Israel had waited for the promised Anointed One to come save them and the whole world from their sins, bad choices, and even death itself. When that moment finally came, a cast of characters witnessed his birth: Joseph, Miriam, the shepherds, and wise men were bystanders to the God-Man who came from the Father overflowing with tender mercy and truth. Celebrate this gift, given to you and the world!

## *An Angel Comes to Joseph*
MATTHEW 1:18-25

This was how Jesus, God's Anointed One, was born.

His mother, Miriam, had promised Joseph to be his wife, *but while she was still a virgin* she became pregnant through the power of the Holy Spirit. Her fiancé, Joseph, was a good man full of integrity and he didn't want to disgrace her, but when he learned of her pregnancy he secretly planned to break the engagement. While he was still debating with himself about what to do, he fell asleep and had a supernatural dream. An angel from the Lord appeared to him in clear light and said, "Joseph, descendant of David, don't hesitate to take Miriam into your home as your wife, because the power of the Holy Spirit has conceived a child in her womb. She will give birth to a son and you are to name him 'Savior,' for he is destined to give his life to save his people from their sins."

This happened so that what the Lord spoke through his prophet would come true:

Listen! A virgin will be pregnant,
she will give birth to a Son,
And he will be known as "Emmanuel,"
which means in Hebrew,

"God became one of us."

When Joseph awoke from his dream, he did all that the angel of the Lord instructed him to do. He took Miriam to be his wife, but they refrained from having sex until she gave birth to her son, whom they named "Jesus."

## The Birth of Jesus
LUKE 2:1–7

During those days, the Roman emperor, Caesar Augustus, ordered that the first census be taken throughout his empire. (Quirinius was the governor of Syria at that time.) Everyone had to travel to his or her hometown to complete the mandatory census. So Joseph and his fiancée, Miriam, left Nazareth, a village in Galilee, and journeyed to their hometown in Judea, to the village of Bethlehem, King David's ancient home. They were required to register there, since they were both direct descendants of David. Miriam was pregnant and nearly ready to give birth.

When they arrived in Bethlehem, Miriam went into labor, and there she gave birth to her firstborn son. After wrapping the newborn baby in strips of cloth, they laid him in a feeding trough since there was no available upstairs room in the village.

## *An Angelic Encounter*
LUKE 2:8-20

That night, in a field near Bethlehem, there were shepherds watching over their flocks. Suddenly, an angel of the Lord appeared in radiant splendor before them, lighting up the field with the blazing glory of God, and the shepherds were terrified! But the angel reassured them, saying, "Don't be afraid. For I have come to bring you good news, the most joyous news the world has ever heard! And it is for everyone everywhere! For today in Bethlehem a rescuer was born for you. He is the Lord Yahweh, the Messiah. You will recognize him by this miracle sign: you will find a baby wrapped in strips of cloth and lying in a feeding trough!"

Then all at once, a vast number of glorious angels appeared, the very armies of heaven! And they all praised God, singing:

Glory to God in the highest realms of heaven!
For there is peace and a good hope given
   to the sons of men.

When the choir of angels disappeared back to heaven, the shepherds said to one another, "Let's go! Let's hurry and find this Manifestation that is born in Bethlehem and see for ourselves what the

Lord has revealed to us." So they ran into the village and found their way to Miriam and Joseph. And there was the baby, lying in a feeding trough.

Upon seeing this miraculous sign, the shepherds recounted what had just happened. Everyone who heard the shepherds' story was astonished by what they were told.

But Miriam treasured all these things in her heart and often pondered what they meant.

The shepherds returned to their flock, ecstatic over what had happened. They praised God and glorified him for all they had heard and seen for themselves, just like the angel had said.

### Baby Jesus Dedicated in the Temple
LUKE 2:21–38

On the day of the baby's circumcision ceremony, eight days after his birth, his parents gave him the name Jesus, the name prophesied by the angel before he was born. After Miriam's days of purification had ended, it was time for her to come to the temple with a sacrifice, according to the laws of Moses after the birth of a son. So Miriam and Joseph took the baby Jesus to Jerusalem to be dedicated before the Lord. For it is required in the law of the Lord, "Every firstborn male shall be a set-apart one for God." And, to offer a prescribed sacrifice, "either a pair of turtledoves or two young pigeons."

As they came to the temple to fulfill this requirement, an *elderly* man was there waiting—a resident of Jerusalem whose name was Simeon. He was a very good man, a lover of God who kept himself pure, and the Spirit of holiness rested upon him. Simeon believed in the imminent appearing of the one called "The Refreshing of Israel." For the Holy Spirit had revealed to him that he would not see death before he saw the Messiah, the Anointed One of God. For this reason the Holy Spirit had moved him to be in the temple court at the very moment Jesus' parents entered to fulfill the requirement of the sacrifice.

Simeon cradled the baby in his arms and praised God and prophesied, saying:

Lord and Master, I am your loving servant,
and now I can die content,
for your promise to me has been fulfilled.
With my own eyes I have seen your Manifestation,
the Savior you sent into the world.
He will be glory for your people Israel,
and the Revelation Light for all people everywhere!

Miriam and Joseph stood there, awestruck over what was being said about their baby.

Simeon then blessed them and prophesied over Miriam, saying:

A painful sword will one day pierce your
inner being,
for your child will be rejected by many in Israel.
And the destiny of your child is this:
He will be laid down as a miracle sign
for the downfall and resurrection of many
in Israel.
Many will oppose this sign, but it will expose to all
the innermost thoughts of their hearts before God.

A prophetess named Anna was also in the temple court that day. She was from the Jewish tribe of Asher and the daughter of Phanuel. Anna was an aged widow who had been married only seven years before her husband passed away. After he died she chose to worship God in the temple continually. For the past eighty-four years she had been serving God with night-and-day prayer and fasting.

While Simeon was prophesying over Miriam and Joseph and the baby, Anna walked up to them and burst forth with a great chorus of praise to God for the child. And from that day forward she told everyone in Jerusalem who was waiting for their redemption that the anticipated Messiah had come!

## *The Wise Men Visit*
MATTHEW 2:1–12

Jesus was born in Bethlehem near Jerusalem during the reign of King Herod. After Jesus' birth a group of spiritual priests from the East came to Jerusalem and inquired of the people, "Where is the child who is born king of the Jewish people? We observed his star rising in the sky and we've come to bow before him in worship."

King Herod was shaken to the core when he heard this, and not only him, but all of Jerusalem was disturbed when they heard this news. So he called a meeting of the Jewish ruling priests and religious scholars, demanding that they tell him where the promised Messiah was prophesied to be born.

"He will be born in Bethlehem, in the land of Judah," they told him. "Because the prophecy states:

And you, little Bethlehem, are not insignificant
Among the clans of Judah, for out of you will
emerge The Shepherd-King of my people Israel!"

Then Herod secretly summoned the spiritual priests from the East to ascertain the exact time the star first appeared. And he told them, "Now go to Bethlehem and carefully look there for the child, and when you've found him, report to me so that I can go and bow down and worship him too."

And so they left, and on their way to Bethlehem, suddenly the same star they had seen in the East reappeared! Amazed, they watched as it went ahead of them and stopped directly over the place where the child was. And when they saw the star, they were so ecstatic that they shouted and celebrated with unrestrained joy. When they came into the house and saw the young child with Miriam, his mother, they were overcome. Falling to the ground at his feet they worshiped him. Then they opened their treasure boxes full of gifts and presented him with gold, frankincense, and myrrh. Afterward they returned to their own country by another route because God had warned them in a dream not to go back to Herod.

### The Living Expression
JOHN 1:1–5, 9–14

> In the very beginning the Living Expression
>    was already there
> And the Living Expression was with God,
>    yet fully God.
> They were together—face to face, in the very
>    beginning.
> And through his creative inspiration
> this Living Expression made all things,
> for nothing has existence apart from him!

Life came into being because of him,
for his life is light for all humanity.
And this Living Expression is the Light
    that bursts through gloom—
the Light that darkness could not diminish!
For the Light of Truth was about to come
    into the world
and shine upon everyone.
He entered into the very world he created,
yet the world was unaware.
He came to the very people he created;
to those who should have recognized him,
but they did not receive him.
But those who embraced him and
    took hold of his name
were given authority to become
    the children of God!
He was not born by the joining of human
    parents
or from natural means or by a man's desire,
but he was born of God.
And so the Living Expression
became a man and lived among us!
And we gazed upon the splendor of his glory,
the glory of the One and Only,
who came from the Father overflowing
with tender mercy and truth!

# The
# STORY
## *of*
# *Christmas*

*A* promise is an assurance that someone will do something or that something will happen. The promise of Christmas assures us a number of benefits: God's love and favor cascades over us; we're made right with God; we're liberated from sin's guilt and power; and we have peace with God. Ultimately our Savior lives in us—giving us hope, peace, and joy.

### *The Gospel Reveals God's Righteousness*
ROMANS 3:21–26

But now, independently of the law, the righteousness of God is tangible and brought to light through Jesus, the Anointed One. This is the righteousness that the Scriptures prophesied would come. It is God's righteousness made visible through the faithfulness of Jesus Christ. And now all who believe in him receive that gift. For there is really no difference between us, for we all have sinned and are in need of the glory of God. Yet through his powerful declaration of acquittal, God freely gives away his righteousness. His gift of love and favor now cascades over us, all because Jesus, the Anointed One, has liberated us from the guilt, punishment, and power of sin!

Jesus' God-given destiny was to be the sacrifice to take away sins, and now he is our Mercy Seat because of his death on the cross. We come to him for mercy, for God has made a provision for us to be forgiven by faith in the sacred blood of Jesus. This is the perfect demonstration of God's justice, because until now, he had been so patient—holding back his justice out of his tolerance for us. So he covered over the sins of those who lived prior to Jesus' sacrifice. And when the season of tolerance came to an end, there was only one possible way for God to give away his righteousness and still be true to both his justice and his mercy—to offer up his own Son. So now, because we stand on the faithfulness of Jesus, God declares us righteous in his eyes!

### Made Alive in Christ
EPHESIANS 2:4–10

But God still loved us with such great love. He is so rich in compassion and mercy. Even when we were dead and doomed in our many sins, he united us into the very life of Christ and saved us by his wonderful grace! He raised us up with Christ the exalted One, and we ascended with him into the glorious perfection and authority of the heavenly realm, for we are now joined as one with Christ!

Throughout the coming ages we will be the visible display of the infinite, limitless riches of his grace and kindness, which was showered upon us in Jesus Christ. For it was only through this wonderful grace that we believed in him. Nothing we did could ever earn this salvation, not even our faith, for it was the gracious gift from God that brought us to Christ! So no one will ever be able to boast, for salvation is never a reward for good works or human striving.

We have become his poetry, a re-created people

that will fulfill the destiny he has given each of us, for we are joined to Jesus, the Anointed One. Even before we were born, God planned in advance our destiny and the good works we would do to fulfill it!

### *The Supremacy of the Son of God*
COLOSSIANS 1:15–23

He is the divine portrait, the true likeness of the invisible God, and the firstborn Heir of all creation. For the Son created everything, both in the heavenly realm and on the earth, all that is seen and all that is unseen. Every seat of power, realm of government, principality, and authority—it was all created by him and for his purpose! He existed before anything was made, so now everything finds completion in him.

He is the Head of his body, which is the church. And since he is the Beginning and the Firstborn Heir in resurrection, he must always be embraced as the most exalted One, holding first place in everything. For God is satisfied to have all his fullness dwelling in Christ. And by the blood of his cross, everything in heaven and earth is restored brought back to himself—back to its original intent, restored to innocence again!

Even though you were once distant from him, living in the shadows of your evil thoughts and actions, he reconnected you back to himself. He released his supernatural peace to you through the sacrifice of his own body as the sin-payment on your behalf so that you would dwell in his presence. And now there is nothing between you and Father God, for he sees you as holy, flawless, and restored!

Continue to advance in faith, assured of a firm foundation to grow upon. Never be shaken from the hope of the gospel you have believed in. And this is the glorious news I preach all over the world.

### Jesus Brings Many People to Glory
HEBREWS 2:14–18

Since all his "children" have flesh and blood, so Jesus became human to fully identify with us. He did this, so that he could experience death and annihilate the effects of the intimidating accuser who holds against us the power of death. By embracing death Jesus sets free those who live their entire lives in bondage to the tormenting dread of death. For it is clear that he didn't do this for the angels, but for all the sons and daughters of Abraham. This is why he had to be a Man and take hold of our humanity in every way. He made us his brothers and sisters and became our merciful and faithful King-Priest before God; as the One who removed our sins to make us one with him. He suffered and endured every test and temptation, so that he can help us every time we pass through the ordeals of life.

### *Christ's Eternal Sacrifice*
HEBREWS 10:11–18

Yet every day priests still serve, ritually offering the same sacrifices again and again—sacrifices that can never take away sin's guilt. But when this Priest had offered the one supreme sacrifice for sin for all time he sat down on a throne at the right hand of God, waiting until all his whispering enemies are subdued and turn into his footstool. And by his one perfect sacrifice he made us perfectly holy and complete for all time!

The Holy Spirit confirms this to us by this Scripture, for the Lord says,

> "Afterwards, I will give them this covenant: I will embed my laws into their hearts and fasten my Word to their thoughts."

And then he says,

> "I will not ever again remember their sins and lawless deeds!"

So if our sins have been forgiven and forgotten, why would we ever need to offer another sacrifice for sin?

## *Christ's Humility*
PHILIPPIANS 2:5–11

And consider the example that Jesus, the Anointed One, has set before us. Let his mindset become your motivation.

He existed in the form of God, yet he gave no thought to seizing that alone as his supreme prize. Instead he emptied himself of his outward glory by reducing himself to the form of a lowly Servant. He became human! He humbled himself and became vulnerable, choosing to be revealed as a Man. He listened to the Father and was obedient to everything he heard. He was a perfect example, even in his death—a criminal's death by crucifixion!

Because of that obedience, God exalted him and multiplied his greatness! He has now been given the greatest of all names!

The authority of the name of Jesus causes every knee to bow in reverence! Everything and everyone will one day submit to this name—in the heavenly realm, in the earthly realm, and in the demonic realm. And every tongue will proclaim in every language: "Jesus Christ is Lord Yahweh," bringing glory and honor to God, his Father!

*The*
# STORY
*of*
## Christmas

*E*very good story must come to an end. God's story is no different. But this ending is unlike any other, because it is actually a beginning: it's the moment when our King returns to *finally* make good on his promise to put this broken world back together. One day King Jesus will return to make "everything to be new and fresh." He will be our God and we will be his children—enjoying him, singing his praises, and reigning with him for all eternity!

## *Signs of the End of the Age*
Luke 21:8–19

"Deception will run rampant with many who will appear on the scene, saying I have sent them, or saying about themselves, 'I am the Messiah!' And the doomsday deceivers will say, 'The end of the age is now here!' But listen to me. Don't be fooled by these imposters.

"There will also be many wars and revolutions on every side, with rumors of more wars to come. Don't panic or give in to your fears, for these things are bound to happen. This is still not the end yet."

Jesus continued, "There will be upheavals of every kind. Nations will go to war against each other and kingdom against kingdom—and there will be terrible earthquakes, seismic events of epic proportion, resulting in famines in one place after another. There will be horrible plagues and epidemics, cataclysmic storms on the earth, and astonishing signs and cosmic disturbances in the heavens. But before all of this happens, you will be hunted down and arrested, persecuted by both civil and religious authorities, and thrown into prison. And because you follow me, you will be on trial before kings and governmental leaders as an opportunity to testify to them in my name. Yet determine in your hearts not to prepare for your own defense. Simply speak with the words of wisdom that I will give you that moment, and none of your persecutors will be able to withstand the grace and wisdom that comes from your mouths.

"You can expect betrayal even by your parents, your brothers, your relatives and friends—and yes, some of you will die as martyrs. You will be hated by all because of my life in you. But don't worry. My grace will never desert you or depart from your life. And by standing firm with patient endurance you will find your souls' deliverance."

## More Signs of the End of the Age
MATTHEW 24:11–14

"And many lying prophets will arise, deceiving multitudes and leading them away from the path of truth. There will be such an increase of sin and lawlessness that those whose hearts once burned with passion for God and others will grow cold. But keep your hope to the end and you will experience life and deliverance.

"Yet through it all, this joyful assurance of the realm of heaven's kingdom will be proclaimed all over the world, providing every nation with a demonstration of the reality of God. And after this the end of this age will arrive."

### The Appearing of the Son of Man
MARK 13:24–27

"This is what will take place after that suffering:

'The sun will be darkened
and the moon will reflect no light.
The stars will be falling from the sky
and all the cosmic powers will be shaken.'

"Then they will see the Son of Man appearing in the midst of clouds and revealed with mighty power and great glory. At that time he will send his messengers, who will gather together his beloved chosen ones from every direction—from the ends of the earth to the ends of heaven!"

### Live Always Ready for the King's Appearing
MATTHEW 24:36–44

"Concerning that day and exact hour, no one knows when it will arrive, not even the angels of heaven—only the Father knows. For it will be exactly like it was in the days of Noah when the Son of Man appears. Before the flood, people lived their lives eating, drinking, marrying, and having children. They didn't realize the end was near until Noah entered the ark, and then suddenly, the flood came and took them all away in judgment. It will happen the same way when the Son of Man appears. At that time, two men will be working on the farm; one will be taken away in judgment, the other left. Two women will be grinding grain; one will be taken away in judgment, the other left. This is why you must stay alert: because no one knows the day your Lord will come.

"But realize this: If a homeowner had known what time of night the burglar would come to rob his house, he would have been alert and ready, and not let his house be robbed. So always be ready, alert, and prepared, because at an hour when you're not expecting him, the Son of Man will come."

## The Judgment of the Multitudes
MATTHEW 25:31–46

"When the Son of Man appears in his majestic glory, with all his angels by his side, he will take his seat on his throne of splendor, and all the nations will be gathered together before him. And like a shepherd who separates the sheep from the goats, he will separate all the people. The 'sheep' he will put on his right side and the 'goats' on his left. Then the King will turn to those on his right and say, 'You have a special place in my Father's heart. Come and experience the full inheritance of the kingdom realm that has been destined for you from before the foundation of the world! For when you saw me hungry, you fed me. When you found me thirsty, you gave me something to drink. When I had no place to stay, you invited me in, and when I was poorly clothed, you covered me. When I was sick, you tenderly cared for me, and when I was in prison you visited me.'

"Then the godly will answer him, 'Lord, when did we see you hungry or thirsty and give you food and something to drink? When did we see you with no place to stay and invite you in? When did we see you poorly clothed and cover you? When did we see you sick and tenderly care for you, or in prison and visit you?'

"And the King will answer them, 'Don't you know? When you cared for one of the least important of these my little ones, my true brothers and sisters, you demonstrated love for me.'

"Then to those on his left the King will say, 'Leave me! For you are under the curse of eternal fire that has been destined for the devil and all his demons. For when you saw me hungry, you refused to give me food, and when you saw me thirsty, you refused to give me something to drink. I had no place to stay, and you refused to take me in as your guest. When you saw me poorly clothed, you closed your hearts and would not cover me. When you saw that I was sick, you didn't lift a finger to help me, and when I was imprisoned, you never came to visit me.'

"And then those on his left will say, 'Lord, when did we see you hungry or thirsty and not give you food and something to drink? When did we see you homeless, or poorly clothed? When did we see you sick and not help you, or in prison and not visit you?'

"Then he will answer them, 'Don't you know? When you refused to help one of the least important among these my little ones, my true brothers and sisters, you refused to help and honor me.' And they will depart from his presence and go into eternal punishment. But the godly and beloved 'sheep' will enter into eternal bliss."

## *The Unopened Scroll*
REVELATION 5:1–14

And I saw the One seated on the throne was holding in his right hand an unopened scroll with writing on the inside and on the outside, and it was sealed with seven seals. Then I saw an incredibly powerful angel proclaiming repeatedly with a great loud voice: "Who is worthy to open the scroll and break its seven seals?" But no person could be found in heaven or on the earth or under the earth that was able to open the scroll and read its contents.

So I broke down weeping; sobbing with sorrow,

because there was no one found who was worthy to break open the scroll and read its contents. Then one of the elders said to me, "Stop weeping, there is One who is worthy! Look! The mighty Lion of Judah's tribe, the root of David—he has conquered! He is the worthy One who can open the scroll and its seven seals."

Then I saw a Lamb standing in the middle of the throne, encircled by the four living creatures and the twenty-four elders. The Lamb had been slaughtered but was now alive! He had seven horns and seven eyes, which are the seven Spirits of God sent out to the ends of the earth! I saw the Lamb approach the throne and he took the scroll from the right hand of the One who sat there. And when the twenty-four elders and the four living creatures saw the Lamb take the scroll, they threw themselves down to the ground at the feet of the Lamb and worshiped Him. Each of them had a harp and golden bowls full of sweet fragrant incense—which are the prayers of God's holy lovers. And they were all singing this new song of praise to the Lamb:

"Because you were slaughtered for us,
you are worthy to take the scroll and open
    its seals!
Your blood was the price paid to redeem us!

You have purchased us for God
from every tribal group and language group,
from every people group and nation.
And you have chosen us to serve our God
as a kingdom of priests who reign on the earth!"

Then I looked, and I heard the voices of myriads of angels in circles around the throne, as well as the voices of the living creatures and the elders—the number of them was over 110 million! This angelic choir was singing with thunderous voices:

"Worthy is the Lamb who was slaughtered
to receive great power and wealth
and wisdom and might
and honor and glory and praise!"

Then every living being joined the angelic choir! Every creature in heaven and on earth, under the earth, in the sea and everything in them were singing in unison:

"Praise, honor, glory and dominion
be to God-Enthroned and to the Lamb
forever and ever!"

Then the four living creatures responded with saying: "AMEN!" And the twenty-four elders threw themselves facedown to the ground and worshiped!

## *A New Heaven and a New Earth*
REVELATION 21:1–7

Then in a vision I saw a new heaven and a new earth! The first heaven and earth had disappeared and the sea no longer existed. And I saw the Holy City, the New Jerusalem, descending out of the heavenly realm from the presence of God, like a bride that had been prepared for the one who will be her husband, adorned for her wedding!

And I heard a thunderous voice from the throne saying, "Look! God's tent is with human beings! And from now on he will live with them in his tabernacle and they all will belong to him. Now God himself will have his home with them—"God-with-them" will be their God! He will wipe away every tear from their eyes and eliminate death entirely! No one will mourn or weep any longer—the pain of wounds will no longer exist, for all of the old order has ceased.

And God-Enthroned spoke to me and said: "Consider this! I am making everything to be new and fresh! Write down at once all that I have told you, because each word is trustworthy and dependable."

Then he said to me, "It is done! For I AM the Alpha and the Omega, the beginning and the end!"

I will give water to all who are thirsty. As my free gift they will continuously drink from the fountain of life-giving water. All who overcome will receive these gifts from me! And I will be their God and they will be my children."

*The*
STORY
*of*
*Christmas*

## Section 5
# TEN PROMISES OF CHRISTMAS

## Hope

*I*n a world of terrorism, recessions, diseases, and poverty, hope is hard to come by these days. Yet the story of Christmas promises just that: hope. The angels declared that with Jesus' birth "there is peace and a good hope given to the sons of men." And Paul frequently reminds us in his letters of our glorious hope because of our belief in Jesus. If you're looking for hope, turn to Jesus and his story!

"Glory to God in the highest realms of heaven! For there is peace and a good hope given to the sons of men."

LUKE 2:14

And this hope is not a disappointing fantasy, because we can now experience the endless love of God cascading into our hearts through the Holy Spirit who lives in us!

ROMANS 5:5

He is given to us like an engagement ring is given to a bride, as the first installment of what's coming! He is our promised hope of a future inheritance for all who have been made alive in Christ. This hope-promise seals us until we have all of redemption's promises and experience complete freedom—all for the supreme glory and honor of God!

EPHESIANS 1:14

Every time we pray for you our hearts overflow with thanksgiving to Father-God, the Father of our Lord Jesus Christ. For we have heard of your devoted lives of faith and the tender love you have for all his holy believers. And from the first time we heard about your conversion until now we faithfully prayed for you, that you would access your destiny through all the treasures of your inheritance stored up in the heavenly realm. For the revelation of the true gospel is as real today as the day you first heard of our glorious hope, now that you have believed in the manifestation of God.

COLOSSIANS 1:3–5

If your faith remains strong, even while surrounded by life's difficulties, you will continue to experience the untold blessings of God! True happiness comes as you pass the test with faith, and receive the victorious crown of life promised to every lover of God!

Every gift God freely gives us is good and perfect, streaming down from the Father of Lights, who shines from the heavens with no hidden shadow or darkness and is never subject to change. God was delight to give us birth by the truth of his infallible Word so that we would fulfill his chosen destiny for us and become the favorite ones out of all his creation!

JAMES 1:12, 17–18

## Peace

In the Bible peace isn't merely the absence of conflict. It's about wholeness, stability, and things being made right. The story of Christmas promises this kind of peace! Jesus tells us he's our refreshing oasis, a refuge for the weary. He also gives us his perfect peace, and makes peace between us and God. With Jesus we have no need to worry, because his story promises our story peace!

"So everyone, come to me! Are you weary, carrying a heavy burden? Then come to me. I will refresh your life, for I am your oasis. Simply join your life with mine. Learn my ways and you'll discover that I'm gentle, humble, easy to please. You will find refreshment and rest in me. For all that I require of you will be pleasant and easy to bear."

MATTHEW 11: 28–30

"I leave the gift of peace with you—my peace. Not the kind of fragile peace given by the world, but my perfect peace. Don't yield to fear or be troubled in your hearts—instead, be courageous!"

JOHN 14:27

Our faith in Jesus transfers God's righteousness to us and he now declares us flawless in his eyes. This means we can now enjoy true and lasting peace with God, all because of what our Lord Jesus, the Anointed One, has done for us.

ROMANS 5:1

For the Messiah has come to preach this sweet message of peace to you, the ones who were distant, and to those who are near. And now, because we are united to Christ and to each other, we both have equal and direct access in the realm of the Holy Spirit to come before the Father!

EPHESIANS 2:17-18

Don't be pulled in different directions or worried about a thing.

Be saturated in prayer throughout each day, offering your faith-filled requests before God with overflowing gratitude. Tell him every detail of your life, then God's wonderful peace that transcends human understanding, will make the answers known to you through Jesus Christ.

PHILIPPIANS 4:6-7

# Joy

There's a difference between joy and happiness. Happiness is often based on situations, people, and things outside ourselves. Joy is another story: it's something internal we can possess regardless of external circumstances. Jesus told us the Holy Spirit fills us with this mystery. Paul explained the Holy Spirit produces it within us. We're also invited to have it—and we can, because it's one of the promises of Christmas.

For the kingdom of God is not a matter of rules about food and drink, but is in the realm of the Holy Spirit, filled with righteousness, peace, and joy.

ROMANS 14:17

But the fruit produced by the Holy Spirit within you is divine love in all its various expressions. This love is revealed through Joy that overflows.

GALATIANS 5:22

Be cheerful with joyous celebration in every season of life. Let joy overflow, for you are united with the Anointed One! Let gentleness be seen in every relationship, for our Lord is ever near.

Don't be pulled in different directions or worried about a thing.

Be saturated in prayer throughout each day, offering your faith-filled requests before God with overflowing gratitude. Tell him every detail of your life, then God's wonderful peace that transcends human understanding, will make the answers known to you through Jesus Christ.

PHILIPPIANS 4:4–7

My fellow believers, when it seems as though you are facing nothing but difficulties see it as an invaluable opportunity to experience all the joy that you can! For you know that when your faith is tested it stirs up power within you to endure all things. And then as your endurance grows even stronger it will release perfection into every part of your being until there is nothing missing and nothing lacking.

JAMES 1:2–4

## Love

The word *love* can be rather empty in substance when it gets used for smart phones and our favorite dessert. When God uses this word, he means it deeply—and shows it! The Bible says God loved us so much that he sent Jesus to us as a gift. Amazingly, God loves his followers in the same way he loves his Son. And the promise of Christmas is that nothing can separate us from this love!

"For this is how much God loved the world—he gave his one and only, unique Son as a gift. So now everyone who believes in him will never perish but experience everlasting life.

"God did not send his Son into the world to judge and condemn the world, but to be its Savior and rescue it! So now there is no longer any condemnation for those who believe in him, but the unbeliever already lives under condemnation because they do not believe in the name of God's beloved Son."

JOHN 3:16–18

"You live fully in me and now I live fully in them
so that they will experience perfect unity,
and the world will be convinced that you have
     sent me.
For they will see that you love each one of them
with the same passionate love that you have
     for me."

JOHN 17:23

Who could ever separate us from the endless love of God's Anointed One? Absolutely no one! For nothing in the universe has the power to diminish his love toward us. Troubles, pressures, and problems are unable to come between us and heaven's love. What about persecutions, deprivations, dangers, and death threats? No, for they are all impotent to hinder omnipotent love, even though it is written:

> All day long we face death threats for your sake,
> God.
> We are considered to be nothing more
> Than sheep to be slaughtered!
>
> ROMANS 8:35–36

If I were fluent in many tongues, even in the tongues of angels, but my heart was not filled with love, then my words are nothing more than irritating noise, like a clanging cymbal. And if I were to have the gift of prophecy and have profound understanding of every mystery, possessing unending supernatural knowledge, and if I had the greatest gift of faith that could move mountains, but have never learned to love others, I am simply nothing. And if I were to be so generous as to give away everything I owned to feed the poor and offer my body to be burned as a martyr, but without the pure motive of love, I gain nothing of value.

Love waits patiently for God's timing. Love is gentle and shows kindness to all. It refuses to be jealous when blessing comes to someone else. Love does not brag about one's achievements nor inflate its own importance. Love does not traffic in shame and disrespect, nor selfishly seek its own honor. Love is not easily irritated or quick to take offense. Love finds delight in the truth, and not in what is wrong. There is nothing loyal-love cannot face, for it never loses faith. It never considers failure to be defeat, for it never gives up.

Love never stops loving. It goes beyond the gift of prophecy, which is temporary. It is more enduring than the gift of tongues, which all will one day fall silent. Love remains long after words of knowledge are forgotten. Now our knowledge and our prophecies are but partial, but when love's perfection arrives, the partial will fade away. When I was a child I spoke about childish matters, for I saw things like a child and my thoughts were that of an immature child. But the day came when I matured, and I set aside my childish ways.

For now we see but a faint reflection as in a mirror, but one day we will see face to face. My understanding is incomplete now, but one day I will understand everything, just as everything about me has been fully understood. Meanwhile, there are three things, which endure: faith, hope, and love—yet love surpasses them all!

1 CORINTHIANS 13:1–8

## Rescue

*N*o one wants to admit it, but we all need help. And actually it's deeper than that: we need to be saved, *rescued*. The letters of Paul remind us we all need rescue from the unwelcome intruders of sin and death. Thankfully, God has helped us by saving us from these powers! Through the power of Jesus and his sacrifice, we are saved from sin and death, released from shame and guilt, and free to serve and worship God.

"He has rescued us from the power of our enemies! This fulfills the sacred oath he made with our father Abraham. Now we can boldly worship God with holy lives, living in purity as priests in his presence every day!"

LUKE 1:73–75

Jesus continued, "In the same way, there will be a glorious celebration in heaven over the rescue of one lost sinner who repents, comes back home, and returns to the fold—more so than for all the righteous people who never strayed away."

LUKE 15:7

What an agonizing situation I am in! So who has the power to rescue this miserable man from the unwelcome intruder of sin and death? I give all my thanks to God, for his mighty power has finally set me free through our Lord Jesus, the Anointed One! So if left to myself, the flesh is aligned with the law of sin, but now my renewed mind is fixed on and submitted to God's righteous principles.

ROMANS 7:24–25

I pray over you a release of the blessings of God's undeserved kindness and total well-being that flows from our Father-God and from the Lord Jesus. He's the Anointed Messiah who offered his soul as the sacrifice for our sins! He has taken us out of this evil world system and set us free through our salvation, just as God desired.

GALATIANS 1:3–4

He has rescued us completely from the tyrannical rule of darkness and has translated us into the kingdom realm of his beloved Son.

COLOSSIANS 1:13

Under the old covenant the blood of bulls, goats, and the ashes of a heifer were sprinkled on those who were defiled and effectively cleansed them outwardly from their ceremonial impurities. Yet how much more will the sacred blood of the Messiah thoroughly cleanse our consciences! For by the power of the eternal Spirit he has offered himself to God as the perfect Sacrifice that now frees us from our dead works to worship and serve the living God.

HEBREWS 9:13–14

✳

## Forgiveness

All of us have a problem stretching all the way back to our ancient ancestors: a sin problem that separates us from God. Yet from the beginning God provided a way for those sins to be forgiven— first through animal sacrifices, then through the sacrifice of his own Son. That's one of the promises of Christmas: our sins cancelled, our ransom paid in full, our sins erased completely. God's forgiveness is one promise you can trust!

Jesus, knowing their thoughts, said to them, "Why do you argue in your hearts over what I do and think that it is blasphemy for me to say his sins are forgiven? Let me ask you, which is easier to prove: when I say, 'Your sins are forgiven,' or when I say,

'Stand up, carry your stretcher, and walk'?" Jesus turned to the paraplegic man and said, "To prove to you all that I, the Son of Man, have the lawful authority on earth to forgive sins, I say to you now, stand up! Carry your stretcher and go on home, for you are healed."

LUKE 5:22–24

The very next day John saw Jesus coming to him to be baptized, and John cried out, "Look! There he is—God's Lamb! He will take away the sins of the world!"

JOHN 1:29

Here's what David says:

"What happy fulfillment is ahead for those
whose rebellion has been forgiven
and whose sins are covered by blood.
What happy progress comes to them
when they hear the Lord speak over them,
'I will never hold your sins against you!'"

ROMANS 4:7–8

Since we are now joined to Christ, we have been given the treasures of salvation by his blood—the total cancellation of our sins—all because of the cascading riches of his grace.

EPHESIANS 1:7

For in the Son all our sins are cancelled and we have the release of redemption through the ransom price he paid—his very blood.

COLOSSIANS 1:14

This "realm of death" describes our former state, for we were held in sin's grasp. But now, we've been resurrected out of that "realm of death" never to return, for we are forever alive and forgiven of all our sins!

And through the divine authority of his cross, he cancelled out every legal violation we had on our record and the old arrest warrant that stood to indict us. He erased it all—our sins, our stained soul, and our shameful failure to keep his laws—he deleted it all and they cannot be retrieved! Everything we once were in Adam has been placed onto his cross and nailed permanently there as a public display of cancellation.

COLOSSIANS 2:13–14

## Freedom

What is that one struggle in your life you can't seem to shake? Maybe it's fear, anger, or an addiction. Did you know one of the promises of Christmas is freedom—from fear, anger, and addiction? Jesus came to bring freedom for the brokenhearted; free us from sin and guilt; and set us free from the curse of the law. The next time you celebrate Jesus' birth, celebrate the gift of regal freedom through the gift of perfect righteousness!

"The Spirit of the Lord is upon me, and he has anointed me to be hope for the poor, freedom for the brokenhearted, and new eyes for the blind, and to preach to prisoners, 'You are set free!' I have come to share the message of Jubilee, for the time of God's great acceptance has begun."

LUKE 4:18–19

"Everyone who believes in him is set free from sin and guilt—something the law of Moses had no power to do."

ACTS 13:39

Death once held us in its grip, and by the blunder of one man, death reigned over humanity. But now we are held in the grip of grace and reign as kings in life, enjoying our regal freedom through the gift of perfect righteousness in the one and only Jesus, the Messiah!

ROMANS 5:17

And God is pleased with you, for in the past you were servants of sin, but now your obedience is heart deep, and your life is being molded by truth through the teaching you are devoted to. And now you celebrate your freedom from your former master—sin. You've left its bondage, and now God's perfect righteousness holds power over you as his loving servants.

ROMANS 6:17–18

Yet, Messiah, our Anointed Substitute, paid the full price to set us free from the curse of the law. He absorbed it completely as he became a "curse" in our place. For it is written:

"Everyone who is hung upon a tree is doubly cursed."

GALATIANS 3:13

But the Scriptures make it clear that since we were all under the power of sin, we needed Jesus! And he is the Savior who brings the kingdom realm to those who believe.

So until the revelation of faith for salvation was released, the Law was a jailor, holding us as prisoners under lock and key until the "faith," which was destined to be revealed, would set us free.

GALATIANS 3:22–23

## Acceptance

It's not often we're known, understood, and accepted for who we are. Yet the story of Christmas offers every person on the planet such a promise! Amazingly, Jesus himself accepts us by offering us his intimate friendship. In our relationship with him we are given full acceptance into the family of God. We are his children, his darlings! If you've been searching for acceptance, turn to the story of Christmas.

"I have never called you 'servants,' because a master doesn't confide in his servants, and servants don't always understand what the master is doing. But I call you my most intimate friends, for I reveal to you everything that I've heard from my Father."

JOHN 15:15

And you did not receive the "spirit of religious duty," leading you back into the fear of never being good enough. But you have received the "Spirit of Full Acceptance," enfolding you into the family of God. And you will never feel orphaned, for as he rises up within us, our spirits join him in saying the words of tender affection, "Beloved Father, Abba!"

ROMANS 8:15

Remember the prophecy God gave in Hosea:

"To those who were rejected
and not my people, I will say to them:
'You are mine.'
And to those who were unloved I will say:
'You are my darling.'"

ROMANS 9:25

Now we're no longer living like slaves under the law, but we enjoy being God's very own sons and daughters! And because we're his, we can access everything our Father has—for we are one with Jesus the Anointed One!

GALATIANS 4:7

## Purpose

People spend their whole lives searching for the meaning and purpose of life. What they don't realize is that it's been right in front of them the whole time. Christmas offers us the promise of experiencing the meaning of life, because in Christ we are invited to fulfill God's designed purpose. Through a relationship with Jesus we discover what God has destined for us to do before we were born. The story of Christmas is where you discover who you really are!

So we are convinced that every detail of our lives is continually woven together to fit into God's perfect plan of bringing what is good into our lives, for we are his lovers who have been invited to fulfill his designed purpose.

ROMANS 8:28

Before we were even born, he gave us our destiny; that we would fulfill the plan of God who always accomplishes every purpose and plan in his heart.

EPHESIANS 1:11

Throughout the coming ages we will be the visible display of the infinite, limitless riches of his grace and kindness, which was showered upon us in Jesus Christ. For it was only through this wonderful grace that we believed in him. Nothing we did could ever earn this salvation, not even our faith, for it was the gracious gift from God that brought us to Christ! So no one will ever be able to boast, for salvation is never a reward for good works or human striving.

We have become his poetry, a re-created people that will fulfill the destiny he has given each of us, for we are joined to Jesus, the Anointed One. Even before we were born, God planned in advance our destiny and the good works we would do to fulfill it!

EPHESIANS 2:7–10

So here's my dilemma: Each day I live means bearing more fruit in my ministry; yet I fervently long to be liberated from this body and joined fully to Christ. That would suit me fine, but the greatest advantage to you would be that I remain alive. So you can see why I'm torn between the two.

Yet deep in my heart I'm confident that I will be spared so I can add to your joy and further strengthen and mature your faith. When I am freed to come to you, my deliverance will give you a reason to boast even more in Jesus Christ alone.

PHILIPPIANS 1:22–26

## Victory

Sometimes life can be defeating. We fail an important test, give in to temptation, or lose a close friend. The final promise of Christmas reminds us, though, that through Jesus we've got the victory! Jesus tells us that right now we live in joyous freedom;

that God has not condemned us, he is for us; and that at the end of the age we will be rewarded a hundred fold. Christmas offers us the victorious life as a gift.

Jesus responded, "Listen to the truth: In the age of the restoration of all things, when the Son of Man sits on his glorious throne, you who have followed me will have twelve thrones of your own, and you will govern the twelve tribes of Israel. For anyone who has left behind their home and property, leaving family—brothers or sisters, mothers or fathers, or children—for my sake, they will be repaid a hundred times over and will inherit eternal life. "

MATTHEW 19:28–29

But now, as God's loving servants, you live in joyous freedom from the power of sin. So consider the benefits you now enjoy—you are brought deeper into the experience of true holiness that ends with eternal life! For sin's meager wages is death, but God's lavish gift is life eternal, found in your union with our Lord Jesus, the Anointed One.

ROMANS 6:22–23

If God has determined to stand with us, tell me, who then could ever stand against us? For God has proved his love by giving us his greatest treasure, the gift of his Son. And since God freely offered him up as the sacrifice for us all, he certainly won't withhold from us anything else he has to give.

Who then would dare to accuse those whom God has chosen in love to be his? God himself is the judge who has issued his final verdict over them—"Not guilty!"

Who then is left to condemn us? Certainly not Jesus, the Anointed One! For he gave his life for us, and even more than that, he has conquered death and is now risen, exalted, and enthroned by God at his right hand. So how could he possibly condemn us since he is continually praying for our triumph?

ROMANS 8:31–34

And since you've been united to Jesus Christ the Messiah, you are now Abraham's "child" and inherit all the promises of the kingdom-realm!

GALATIANS 3:29

# The
# STORY
## *of*
# *Christmas*

*D*o you know who was the first person to receive Christmas presents? Jesus! After his birth a group of wise men came to worship him. They gave him three expensive gifts: gold, frankincense, and myrrh. These gifts symbolized Jesus' deity—holiness, excellence, and devotion—and the suffering love that would lead him to die on the cross for humanity. Perhaps we should say *we* were the first ones to receive a Christmas gift!

"For this is how much God loved the world," one of Jesus' followers wrote, "he gave his one and only, unique Son as a gift." That includes you! And just as every gift offers a promise when it's unwrapped, "everyone who believes in him will never perish but experience everlasting life" (John 3:16).

When you unwrap the story of Christmas, you receive the promises of Christmas: forgiveness from sins, release from shame and guilt, peace with God, and unending life. If you'd like to receive the gift of Jesus and all that he means for life, say a prayer like this to God:

God, I have sinned against you. I am truly sorry and I turn from my way of doing things. For the sake of Jesus have mercy on me and forgive me.

Jesus, I believe you died for me, and I thank you for your sacrifice. I believe you paid the price for my sins, and I trust your payment for my rescue. I believe God raised you from the dead, and I need that new life myself.

God, I give you my life. Fill me with your Spirit and help me live for you all my days. Amen.

With this prayer you have begun your walk with Jesus and are now part of God's family. Welcome, and begin enjoying and living the story of Christmas!

This is a gospel of miracles and there is a freshness and vigor about Mark that is gripping to the reader. As the briefest of the four gospels, you will enjoy reading of Jesus' supreme power over both the invisible and visible worlds. He is Master over creation, man, and the devil, for he is the perfect Servant who came to do the Father's will. Mercy triumphs in every page of the gospel of Mark. You will fall in love with this splendid Man, Jesus Christ, as you read this inspired account of his life.

Do you want to discover the heavenly treasures of faith, grace, true righteousness, and power? Plug into the book of Romans and you'll never be the same again. Gifts and glory are waiting for you to unwrap and make your own. Live the truths of Romans and watch how God's love sets you free!

Also included is an eight-week Bible study that complements *Romans: Grace and Glory*. For individuals and small groups, each lesson will help you encounter, explore, and share the heart of God, drawing you closer and deeper into his passionate heart for you.

# Coming Spring 2016

Many errors had crept into the Corinthians' belief system and spiritual walk. In his first letter Paul addressed issues including living godly lives even in a corrupt culture; being unified as one body without competition; maintaining sexual and moral purity; understanding the role of spiritual gifts; embracing love as the greatest virtue that must live within our hearts; maintaining orderly worship with proper respect toward one another; keeping the hope of the resurrection burning brightly in our hearts; and more. We can also receive encouragement as he told them they possessed every spiritual gift, fully equipped to minister to others, and that they were capable of demonstrating love to all. Their hope of a future resurrection brings meaning to our lives today.

2 Corinthians is one of the most personal and intimate of all of Paul's epistles. He opens his heart to the church of Corinth and tells them secrets of his miracle encounters with Jesus and instructs them in how to live in one continual triumph after another. The victory of Christ shines through both of Paul's letters to the Corinthians. It will change you life and enrich your faith to be all that God has destined you to be. Read it and be transformed!

# About The Passion Translation

The Passion Translation Bible is a new, heart-level translation that expresses God's fiery heart of love to this generation, using Hebrew, Greek, and Aramaic manuscripts and merging the emotion and life-changing truth of God's Word.

God longs to have his Word expressed in every language in a way that unlocks the passion of his heart. The goal of this work is to trigger inside every reader an overwhelming response to the truth of the Bible, unfolding the deep mysteries of the Scriptures in the love language of God, the language of the heart.

If you are hungry for God and want to know him on a deeper level, The Passion Translation will help you encounter God's heart and discover what he has for your life.

For information about all books in The Passion Translation and future releases, please visit

www.thepassiontranslation.com